SHAMELESS AUDACITY

21-DAY DEVOTIONAL

Carolyn Olson

SHAMELESS AUDACITY

21-Day Devotional

Independently Published

Carolyn Olson

Unless otherwise noted, all scriptures referenced in this devotional are taken from The Holy Bible, New International Version® NIV® Copyright © 1973, 1978, 1984, 2011 by Biblica®, Inc.

ISBN: 9781976852787

TheCarolynOlson.com

Where you're at, is not where you have to stay.

Ken Hubbard, Pastor of Radius Church

Contents

Carolyn Olson

FORWARD
BY KEN HUBBARD

Often when we see success, we look at what that person is doing and try to mimic it to get the same results. Often, however, I have found that it's what we don't see that creates the most success.

Matthew 6:6
But when you pray, go into your room, close the door and pray to your Father, who is unseen. Then your Father, who sees what is done in secret, will reward you.

A short time after we launched Radius church I met Carolyn Olson. Within a couple of months, she launched our prayer ministry which consisted mostly of her praying alone in a stage closet by herself. Over the following year we watched our church grow and God's favor show up in a multitude of ways.

In our society we like to elevate the leader and analyze the systems to see why there has been success. While leadership and systems are important we know that...

Unless the Lord builds the house, the builders labor in vain.

Unless the Lord watches over the city, the guards stand watch in vain.

As we launched our second location, we knew it needed to be covered in prayer. Once again Carolyn and her team led the charge with 21 days of prayer leading the launch. You are now holding in your hand the map she used to direct our teams at Radius.

I have heard it said that it takes 21 days to create a habit. Use this devotional as a guide for the next 21 days and then start over, again and again. Let it be the catalyst that causes you to show up and meet with God. If you show up, God will too.

When we look at the life of Daniel, we gain insight and understanding into the significance of 21 days:

Daniel 10:12-13
Then he continued, "Do not be afraid, Daniel. Since the first day that you set your mind to gain understanding and to humble yourself before your God, your words were heard, and I have come in response to them. But the prince of the Persian kingdom resisted me twenty-one days. Then Michael, one of the chief princes, came to help me, because I was detained there with the king of Persia.

I challenge you to start the journey of prayer and create the habit of meeting with God. You might be 21 days away from your biggest breakthrough. If you show up, God will too.

DAY 1 – DECIDE TO WALK WITH GOD

This decision is more than just accepting Jesus Christ as your personal Savior. That is the first step. Turning away from sin and receiving the gift of salvation is a fantastic experience guaranteeing the promise of eternal life. But that should be only the first step in your journey with our Lord Jesus.

Too many new Christians merely add God to their existing life without changing anything. They go about the business of living, adding Sunday morning church to their lives, yet wondering why they can't find the peace they expected. They hear scriptures quoted in church about living a life of abundance and wonder why they don't have it. After a while, they usually get fed up with the Christian hype and abandon church altogether.

Make an intentional decision to follow hard after God. If you want all of God, He needs all of you. It's not just going to happen. As with everything in life, it is a conscious decision. Every day we all get to decide what will fill our life. Including God in your day is a choice. Choosing to read His Word and spend a few minutes in prayer is a choice, which can become a habit. And what a wonderful habit it is! The more time you spend with God, the more He becomes your Lord. As your relationship with Him grows, you will suddenly realize that you long for that time spent with Him in His Word or in prayer.

Romans 12:11 says, *"Never be lacking in zeal, but keep your spiritual fervor, serving the Lord."* The zeal you felt that first day you received Christ should remain with you. But just as a fire will eventually go out without tending, you must tend to your relationship with God. Colossians 2:6 says, *"So then, just as you received Christ Jesus as Lord, continue to live your lives in him."* Continue living your lives IN HIM!

Bible Reading Plan: Psalm 139

Prayer Focus: As you begin to spend time with the Lord today, ask Him to come into your life again. Whether you've been walking closely with the Lord for years, or are a new Christian, invite Him into your life to reveal His Nature, His Thoughts to you. Use this time to reflect on the Lord and all the goodness He's brought to your life. Even if you are in a valley right now, as long as you have breath, there is something good to see in Him.

DAY 2 – CREATE SPACE FOR GOD IN YOUR LIFE

etermine to create space for God in your life. After making the intentional decision to give your life to God, you must give Him space, so He can fill it. Do not overthink this – just make room for Him. Matthew 6:6 says, *"But when you pray, go into your room, close the door and pray to your Father, who is unseen. Then your Father, who sees what is done in secret, will reward you."* Get alone with God. Carve out space and time to be with Him every day.

If you are new to praying, then start with 3 minutes. Find a quiet place, set your timer for 3 minutes, and just start talking to Jesus. Say whatever is on your mind. Tell Him about your day, your cares, your innermost thoughts. By giving the Lord space in your life, even just 3 minutes, you are showing God you sincerely want Him in your life. Maybe you've been a Christian for a long while yet still seek more of Him. Then, commit to reading His Word for a few minutes every day in addition to praying for a few minutes. Carve out that time and place for the next 20 days and give Him all of yourself during that time.

You see, it all starts with taking one step closer to Him. If you take one step closer to God, He'll move closer to you. James 4:8 *"Draw near to God, and he will draw near to you."*

Don't let religion in the past hinder your new-found walk with God. Remember when Jesus died on that cross, the curtain of the temple tore in two from top to bottom. The torn curtain meant that everyone now has access to God our Father; we no longer need an earthly priest to represent us before God. We come boldly to His Throne, and He fills that empty place inside us that only He can fill. Don't just add God to your life. Create room for Him to fill you completely.

Bible Reading Plan: Psalm 119

(Note: Jesus fulfilled the law. When you read "law", "statutes" or "decrees", try replacing those words with Jesus. For we alone can't obey the law, but only through Jesus.)

Prayer Focus: Renew your commitment of time to the Lord. As you draw near to the Lord today, ask Him to fill the new-found space you've created. As you consider His Word today, ask Him to open your heart to understand the scriptures in a new way. In fact, praying the Word of God is a sure way to know you are praying within the Will of God. Pray Psalm 86:1-13 from your heart, and He will be sure to answer it.

Carolyn Olson

DAY 3 – SURRENDER YOUR LIFE TO GOD

Choose to surrender your life to God. Yield your whole life to Him realizing that He is more than able to care for you. He's already provided everything you need to live your life as a victor, not a victim of your circumstances. The first step to receiving the victor's crown is to surrender it all to Him.

Many people are afraid to yield their lives to God for fear of losing control. But it's just the opposite! By NOT surrendering your whole life to God, you have no control over your life. The Bible says that Satan is the god of this world. With Satan being in control of this world, we face trials and difficulties that threaten to overwhelm us and cause us to stumble in our walk with God. Once you realize that your life is not your own, and you surrender it all to Him, His Grace and Mercy set you free from the chains of the enemy. Matthew 16:24-25 says, *"Then Jesus said to his disciples, 'Whoever wants to be my disciple must deny themselves and take up their cross and follow me. For whoever wants to save their life will lose it, but whoever loses their life for me will find it.'"*

It's only by surrendering your whole life to the Lord that you have control. When you surrender and begin to recognize who you are in Christ and learn of the authority in that Name, the devil will be on the run. Yes, trials and difficulties will still come your way. But your response to those circumstances will begin to change, and you will find yourself the victor every time. The days of being a victim to the circumstances of your life are over, once you realize who you are in Christ. Lay it all down for Him who is more than able to give you life, and life abundantly.

But what does it mean to surrender your life to God? What does that look like? Many people say they have surrendered and given their lives to God, yet still are overwhelmed by worry and anxiety. Surrendering to God, yielding everything to Him and denying themselves means a complete dependence on the Lord. When worry or anxiety come, you refuse to pick it up instead resting on the Word of God. Luke 10:19 says, *"I have given you authority to trample on snakes and scorpions and to overcome all the power of the enemy; nothing will harm you."* Believe His Word. We have been given authority to overcome all the power of the enemy and nothing will harm us. Nothing will harm us! By surrendering all to God, you are receiving the authority as promised in His Word. Thus, you have more control over every trial and storm in your life as you rest on His Promises.

Bible Reading Plan: Psalm 40

Prayer Focus: As you come before the Lord today, once again give your whole heart to the Lord. Invite Him to take control of your life, surrendering your will and choosing to yield control to Him who is more than able to care for you. As you seek Him first and take this beginning step to put Him first in your life, go ahead and remind Him all that you are entrusting to Him. Lay it all down at His feet. Give to Him your family, your job, your finances, your health, your hopes, and your dreams knowing that His Word promises to care for you.

Carolyn Olson

DAY 4 – PARTICIPATE IN A RELATIONSHIP WITH GOD

Participate in a relationship with God. Relationships are a two-way street. You wouldn't be good friends with someone if you never talked to each other. If one person does all the talking, it is not a very fulfilling relationship. Your marriage would suffer if you never made time for each other. If you never spent time with your children, there would be no closeness and no relationship. To have a fulfilling relationship with the Lord requires that you participate in the relationship with Him, taking the time to get to know Him.

Reading His Word is a great way to start getting to know God. If you want to know Him, read His Word. As you think about His Word, just talk to Him about it. The primary goal of prayer is to build a relationship with God. If you come from a religious background, you might need to renew your thinking about your relationship with God. Remember that as believers, we are children of God and should come to Him as the dear children that we are.

Bring every care, concern and thought to Him in prayer never worrying if you are saying the wrong thing. There is nothing you can say in prayer that is wrong if you are praying with a right heart yearning for a closer relationship with Him. He is a big God and can handle everything you bring to Him with a sincere desire in your heart to know Him more.

Ephesians 1: 4-5 (NCV) says, *"That is, in Christ, he chose us before the world was made so that we would be his holy people—people without blame before him. Because of his love, God had already decided to make us his own children through Jesus Christ. That was what he wanted and what pleased him,"* God created us to be His children. We are his sons and daughters, and like a good Father, He desires to have a relationship with us. And like a good Father, He won't push or shove His way into our lives. Instead, He waits for us to come to Him. Once we turn to Him, He's right there with open arms to receive us and shower us with His blessing.

Bible Reading Plan: Ephesians 1

Prayer Focus: As you draw near to the Lord today with a sincere heart, ask Him to reveal Himself to you in new ways. The prayer in Ephesians 1:16-19 is a great prayer to say for yourself and your loved ones. Make it personal! Keep asking that our glorious Father give you a Spirit of wisdom and revelation, so that you would know Him more. Keep asking that He open the eyes of your heart so that you know the hope of your calling in Him, so that you know your glorious inheritance in Him, and that you know the great power that is for us who believe.

Carolyn Olson

DAY 5 – MAKE THE WORD OF GOD PARAMOUNT IN YOUR LIFE

Resolve to make the Word of God the final word in your life. If you've made a commitment to walk with God and made space in your life for Him, then reading the Word of God should become as necessary to you as breathing. Most people think that the need for air is based on your body's intense desire for oxygen. Instead, the need to breath is based on the body's intense desire to exhale, to get rid of the toxic waste of carbon dioxide. Likewise, as we walk with God, our desire to be close to Him will reflect an intense need to get rid of toxic things in our life, immediately followed by the desire for His life-giving Word.

John 1:1 says, *"In the beginning was the Word, and the Word was with God, and the Word was God."* The Word *was God*! If you want to know God, look to His Word. If you want to know what God says about your circumstances, look to His Word. For every circumstance, trial, difficulty, suffering, worry, pain or disease – there is a scripture for it. God has something to say to you about your current circumstances. Look to His Word, and decide in your heart to believe it. There's no magic about it. Intense study isn't needed to take God at His Word. Simply choose to believe every word written in His Book, and receive it for your life.

Isaiah 55:11 says, "*So is my word that goes out from my mouth: It will not return to me empty, but will accomplish what I desire and achieve the purpose for which I sent it.*" You can take God at His Word. If He says he'll do something in His Word, He'll do it. God's Word works!

Psalm 119:89 says, "*Your word, Lord, is eternal; it stands firm in the heavens.*" His Word is everlasting, an unshakable foundation for your every problem. Psalm 119:105 says, "*Your word is a lamp for my feet, a light on my path.*" Think of the lamp shining on the dim path in front of you. Unlike a flashlight of today, a lamp only shines its' light a few steps in front of you. It only makes sense that the Lord will shine His Light along our paths a few steps, so we learn to trust Him. We won't ever see the end of the path, but He's right there with His Word saying to you, 'Trust Me and take a step.' When you don't know the way you should go, look to His Word.

According to Romans 10:17, "*Faith comes from hearing the message, and the message is heard through the word about Christ.*" There is no shortcut to building your faith. To build your faith, get more of the Word in you.

Bible Reading Plan: Ephesians 3

Prayer Focus: As you seek the Lord today, commit in your heart to believe everything in His Word. Ask the Lord to help you with any unbelief, and choose to accept Him at His Word fully. Make Paul's prayer for the Ephesians the cry of your heart. Ask that He strengthen you with power, by His Spirit, in your inner being, so that Christ dwells in your heart through faith. Ask that the Lord give you the power to grasp the truly vast love of Christ, and to know this love that surpasses understanding, so that you would be filled to the measure of all the fullness of God. Reflect on that promise and what that would mean for you, filled to the fullest measure of God.

Carolyn Olson

DAY 6 – CELEBRATE WHO YOU ARE IN CHRIST

It's time to get excited about who we are in Christ Jesus! Countless times in the scripture we are told who we are in Him. Galatians 3:26 says, "*So in Christ Jesus you are all children of God through faith.*" In Him, we are children of God!

Think about that for just a minute, reflect on what that means. You are a son or daughter of the Most High God! You may not have had a good relationship with your earthly father, or didn't know him at all. Even if you had a loving earthly dad in your life, there is always a longing for acceptance and love from him. How much more, oh how MUCH MORE does our Father in Heaven love us that He not only wants to, but already has, given us everything we need to live a life of abundance.

2 Corinthians 5:21 says, "*God made him who had no sin to be sin for us, so that in him we might become the righteousness of God.*" In Him, we are the righteousness of God. It's nothing we do, not our works

that earned it, but Christ's sacrifice for us purchased our righteousness.

Ephesians 1:3 says, "*Praise be to the God and Father of our Lord Jesus Christ, who has blessed us in the heavenly realms with every spiritual blessing in Christ.*" In Him, we are blessed in the heavenly realms with every spiritual blessing. EVERY spiritual blessing in Christ! It's time we learned what spiritual blessings belong to us.

Galatians 3 is a good place to start. Verse 9 states, "*So those who rely on faith are blessed along with Abraham, the man of faith.*" And verse 14 says, "*He redeemed us in order that the blessing given to Abraham might come to the Gentiles through Christ Jesus, so that by faith we might receive the promise of the Spirit.*"

In Him, we are children of God and the righteousness of God. As the righteous children of God, we share an inheritance that has been passed down from Abraham. This inheritance is something to celebrate!

It was never God's intention to leave His children lost, broken, sick and needy struggling through life. It's time to celebrate the abundant blessings that He has bestowed on His children as we receive by faith.

Bible Reading Plan: Deuteronomy 28:1-14

Prayer Focus: Oh, give thanks this day! You are a child of God! Focus on God your father, and how much more your Father in Heaven wants to give you, His child. Ask Him to fill your heart and mind with the deep knowledge of being His child, and gladly receive in your heart all the blessings He wants to give you. According to Deuteronomy 28, name all the blessings that rightfully belong to you, and give thanks.

DAY 7 – PRAY IN THE NAME OF JESUS

Jesus taught his disciples to pray in Matthew 6: The Lord's Prayer. It's a beautiful model for us believers today. Remember though, that Jesus was teaching his disciples to pray this way while He was still with them. He also taught his disciples to pray IN HIS NAME. In Romans 8:34 we're told that Jesus sits at the right hand of God interceding for us. John 14:12-13 says, "*Very truly I tell you, whoever believes in me will do the works I have been doing, and they will do even greater things than these, because I am going to the Father. And I will do whatever you ask in my name, so that the Father may be glorified in the Son.*"

Consider this the Power of Attorney, given to us through Christ Jesus Himself, and take Him at His Word. Choose to believe that Jesus said what he meant, and meant what He said. A power of attorney is the authority to act for another person about specified matters. Jesus has given us the authority to act on His behalf, in matters specified in His Word. Anything you ask in the precious Name of Jesus, it will be yours. Still not convinced?

John 15:7 says, "*If you remain in me and my words remain in you, ask whatever you wish, and it will be done for you.*" The only requirement is that we remain in Him and His Words remain in us. For if His Word is burning in our hearts, we will be ever mindful to stay in Him. Praying the Will of God, asking for the Will of God is easy because it's all right there in scripture.

Still not convinced? John 15:16 says, "*You did not choose me, but I chose you and appointed you so that you might go and bear fruit—fruit that will last—and so that whatever you ask in my name the Father will give you.*" John 16:23-24 says, "*In that day you will no longer ask me anything. Very truly I tell you, my Father will give you whatever you ask in my name. Until now you have not asked for anything in my name. Ask and you will receive, and your joy will be complete.*"

It's all right there in black and white, yet somehow believers have missed it. Ask in the Name of Jesus so that our joy may be complete.

Bible Reading Plan: John 14

Prayer Focus: Approach the Lord today asking that He reveal this Power of Attorney to you deep in your heart, moving this information from head knowledge to heart knowledge. Ask Him to show His Will to you in scripture so that your prayers, your requests, will have the power of the Name of Jesus, strengthening your faith as you see your prayers answered again and again. Step out in faith and boldly ask for the blessings given to you in Deuteronomy 28, declaring them yours in the Name of Jesus.

Carolyn Olson

DAY 8 – FORGIVE, AND THE LORD WILL FORGIVE YOU

Decide to forgive those who have hurt you. Matthew 6:14 says, *"For if you forgive other people when they sin against you, your heavenly Father will also forgive you."* The Bible is clear that we need to forgive those who abuse us. Forgive those who hurt you, so the Lord will forgive you and hear your prayers. That's right. If you don't forgive, not only do you risk the Lord not forgiving you, but your prayers are hindered. Mark 11:25 says, *"And when you stand praying, if you hold anything against anyone, forgive them, so that your Father in heaven may forgive you your sins."*

To use the authority of the Name of Jesus, and expect results, we must abide in Him, and His Word abide in us. If His Word abides in us, then we must forgive others, so our prayers are heard. No matter how big the offense, it is nothing compared to the offense your sin was to God. If God can forgive you, by the power of God, you can forgive.

But how? How can we possibly forgive those that have hurt us, cheated on us, lied to us, broken their promises to us, stolen our children from us, abused our loved ones, raped us, stabbed us, stolen from us, grieved us, despised us, broken us...how can we possibly forgive?!

It is a simple decision. Just as deciding to follow hard after God, choosing to give your life to the Lord, and starting to pray or read His Word each day is a decision, deciding to forgive someone begins with choosing to do it. You don't even have to want to do it, but the Lord needs a heart willing to obey. So first, decide to forgive that person.

Now, this doesn't mean you'll feel different. When you take the first antibiotic pill for an infection, do you feel different immediately? No. But the first step to eliminating the infection was a decision to take the antibiotic. The first step to forgiving someone is deciding to do it.

Know that once you take that first step, the enemy of your soul will come to try to take it from you. The devil comes to steal, kill and destroy you. (John 10:10) And he'll start reminding you of every thought and feeling that offense brought to your life. So how can you combat the feelings of unforgiveness and remain in your decision to follow hard after God?

James 4:7 says, "*Submit yourselves, then, to God. Resist the devil, and he will flee from you.*" RESIST! That is an active word, and it means that you must do something. Stand against the devil, and oppose him. But how? Speak the Word. Say to the devil that you resist him and tell him to flee, in the Name of Jesus. Remember, you have the

Power of Attorney, and the devil must obey when you use it. When those thoughts and feelings are whispered to you, say, "I refuse to think about that! I resist you, devil! I chose to forgive_____, and I know that God in Heaven forgives me. I refuse to accept anything less than God's best for me." Start declaring who you are in Christ, and be assured that those thoughts and feelings of unforgiveness will vanish.

Bible Reading Plan: Mark 11:12-26 and James 4:1-12

Prayer Focus: In prayer today, submit yourself to God. Declare that you want His best for you and in prayer release the unforgiveness that is in your heart. Tell God all about the offense, tell Him exactly what that person did and how it made you feel. Then, ask Him to take it from you and heal the hurt. Tell Him that you forgive the offense. And ask Him to empower you, by His Spirit, to begin to love that person. Ask God to fill you with His love for that person supernaturally, and for the strength to remain in Him.

Carolyn Olson

DAY 9 – SEEK GOD FIRST IN ALL MATTERS

Make a conscious decision to seek God first, above all else. God desires all of you. He desires to provide for you and all your needs. Matthew 6:33 says, *"But seek first his kingdom and his righteousness, and all these things will be given to you as well."* The things referred to here are found in the previous verses and reference food, drink and clothing. Essentially, put God first and He will take care of all your needs.

"Seek first His Kingdom". What is His Kingdom? "Kingdom" used here is the same as used in the Lord's Prayer, "Thy Kingdom come". It means the right or authority to rule or the reign of God. We are to attempt to find the reign of God in our lives. Most people stop right there when they think of this verse. People will paraphrase this verse to say, seek God first then all these things will be done for me. Don't forget about seeking His Righteousness!

Righteousness means His Justification or, in a broad sense, integrity, virtue, purity of life, rightness, the correctness of thinking, feeling and acting. We are called to work towards or attempt to find integrity, virtue, purity of life, rightness, and the correctness of thinking, feeling and acting – and we are called to do this first, above all else. If we do this, then all our needs will be added to us. The word "added" here means to place additional, add again, give more, or increase. So, He won't merely clothe you with rags and give you bread and water. This verse says that He'll more than take care of our needs by increasing measure.

Seeking God first is about honoring God. When we are born again and have the Spirit of God in us, our hearts yearn to follow Him and do His Will. It's not about following the rules of some religion. Instead, our hearts are filled with a longing to do good, and it becomes a "we get to" follow God. However, it is still a decision we must make. The devil is always right there reminding you that you are busy and have no time for God. Or, he says that you're sick and tired and just don't have enough energy for God. As children of God, we need to rise, resist the devil, and choose to honor God first in all that we do. When we wake up each morning, we should *first* greet the Lord. When we sit down for meals, we should *first* thank the Lord for His provision. When we get paid, we should *first* give back to the Lord what is rightfully His. These are <u>not</u> rules to follow, like some religion, but are simply ways to honor Him in all that we do.

Bible Reading Plan: Matthew 6:25-34

Prayer Focus: As you spend time with the Lord today, ask Him to show you those areas where you need to put Him first. If you haven't been putting Him first, sincerely ask forgiveness with all assurance that you will be forgiven and that your sins are as far away from you as the east is from the west. Don't start making huge promises to the Lord or bargains with Him. Simply commit in your heart to put Him first in your schedule, in your family relationships, and in your finances.

DAY 10 – MAKE AN INTENTIONAL DECISION TO HAVE FAITH IN GOD

Be intentional about your faith. Exercising your faith is not something that just happens without thought, although exercising faith should become your habit.

Many have failed to receive what they've asked for in prayer because they based their faith on prayer instead of the Word of God. Some people expect prayer to do for them what God's Word will do for them. Prayer is successful only when based on the Word of God. Mark 11:23-24 says, *"Truly I tell you, if anyone says to this mountain, 'Go, throw yourself into the sea,' and does not doubt in their heart but believes that what they say will happen, it will be done for them. Therefore, I tell you, whatever you ask for in prayer, believe that you have received it, and it will be yours."*

The keys to the Power of Attorney given to you are right here in Mark. The instructions are listed right here. Do you see it? Step 1: Say It. You can't just think it or want it. You must say what it is that you are requesting. Be specific about your requests. What is it exactly that you want God to do for you? Say it. Declare it. And then Step 2: Believe it. Do not doubt that what you've said will come to pass for it's only then that you receive. Step 3: Receive it. Like with any gift, you must take it or receive it. If someone wraps a beautiful gift for you and leaves it on the table with your name on it, it won't open itself. You won't receive that gift unless you do something, like unwrap it. So, too, with God.

Your words, quite literally, determine your future. Romans 10:10 says "*it is with your mouth you profess your faith.*" Read Mark 11:23 again. That which you say will happen, if you believe. Unfortunately, many of us unknowingly choose to believe the lies of the devil instead of the promises of God. As the god of this world, we see the devil's ways everywhere we go. Unknowingly, we hear his whispers that we are unworthy, poor, weak, sick, or the biggest one: that we were just born this way, that's just how we are. No! We must choose to be intentional about increasing our faith, intentional about believing God and taking Him at His Word. Choose to believe everything you read in scripture knowing that the promises are for you today.

All things are possible if you would believe. In the words of Smith Wigglesworth, "There is nothing God cannot do. He will do everything if you would dare to believe." Ignore what you think or feel, and choose only to believe the promises of God.

Bible Reading Plan: Mark 16

Prayer Focus: As you pray today, decide in your heart to believe His Word. Ask the Lord to strengthen you with His Power to understand His Word and to act on His Word in your life. If there is a mountain in your life that needs moving, then name it, and declare it throw into the sea. Then, claim the blessing that rightfully belongs to you in place of that mountain. Spend a few minutes reflecting on His Church, and what it would mean if all God's people would stand up and claim the words of Jesus in Mark 16:17-18 *"these things will accompany those who believe..."* Stand on the Word, and know who you are in Christ.

Carolyn Olson

DAY 11 – BE SPECIFIC WITH THE LORD

Be specific in your prayers and your asking. What is it you want Him to do for you? The blind man in Luke 18:35-43 was specific in his request. First, he cried out *"Jesus, Son of David, have mercy on me!"* And a second time he cried out even louder because those around him told him to be quiet. So, Jesus stopped and asked him, *"What do you want me to do for you?"* Now that he had the Lord's attention, that blind man didn't continue with a general request merely crying out to God. That blind man answered specifically, *"Lord, I want to see."* Notice Jesus' reply, *"Receive your sight; your faith has healed you."*

Jesus didn't need to use any special gift of healing for that blind man to receive his sight. The Lord Jesus commanded that blind man to receive what he requested, even saying that it was that blind man's faith that did it.

Many times, we are so caught up in our emotions and thoughts that we don't know how to make our requests known to God. In our hurt and pain, we cry out to God, "Have mercy!" or "Help me!"

Please don't misunderstand – the Lord can and will respond to these cries, especially for new believers who don't know how to pray. But we are all charged with growing in our faith. We must learn to see our circumstances through God's eyes and be specific in our requests.

If your marriage is in trouble, continually crying out for change won't work. God cannot change the will of people. Praying that your spouse would do this or that is just not scriptural. So, ask God how He sees your marriage and get to the root of the problem, for there you will see precisely what you need to ask. The same is true praying for our children. Getting into God's Word and learning how He sees your children helps you to understand how to pray specifically for your children. If you are sick with disease, a cold, an infection or cancer, look to His Word. How does God see your circumstance? Continually crying out to God asking Him to heal you, although seemingly specific, won't work. Learn what God's Word says about healing, then be specific, believing what you've requested is already yours.

Bible Reading Plan: Luke 11:1-13

Prayer Focus: After spending several minutes praising God, think about what exactly it is that you want from God. What do you want Him to do for you? If you want Him to bless you, then exactly how does that blessing look? Look to His Word to know His Blessings, then apply it to your life. Practice being specific with the Lord and eagerly expect the Lord to respond.

Carolyn Olson

DAY 12 – ALWAYS PRAY AND NEVER GIVE UP

Endeavor to be specific, always pray and never give up. The parable of the persistent widow found in Luke 18 is a powerful reminder for us to never give up in our prayers. The widow was demanding the unjust judge avenge her of her adversary. According to Strong's Concordance, she was asking to be vindicated of Satan. The unjust judge finally granted her request because the widow kept bothering him and essentially wore him out. How much more will our Just Father in Heaven grant to us if we would only keep coming to Him with our request for vindication?

Remember in grade school when some bully would steal your jacket, or your hat, or your lunch money. What did you do? You asked for it back. The bully might ignore you, so you'd ask again. You kept asking, even going to the yard duty or teacher beseeching them to help you get back what was stolen from you.

Well, the devil comes to steal, kill and destroy. When he's attacking you, are you going to ask that he give it back once or twice? If nothing happens, are you going to shrug your shoulders and walk away saying God just doesn't hear your prayers? Unfortunately, many do. Many people, even mature Christians, unknowingly walk away from the promises of God wrongly thinking that the answer must have been 'no'.

We must learn to pray through until it is finished, until you've received your answer. Merely asking God to intervene in your life once is not enough. If you're believing God for a financial miracle, then keep praying about it until you see it, knowing that it's not His Will that you are poor and struggling not able to provide for your family. If you're believing God for salvation for your loved ones, then you wouldn't just pray once and forget it. No, you would keep asking that they come to their senses until it is done knowing that it's His Will that all come to Him.

Many times, we're tripped up in thinking the answers must come in our timeframe or in the way we think it should be answered. Isaiah 55:8-9 says, *"For my thoughts are not your thoughts, neither are your ways my ways, declares the Lord. As the heavens are higher than the earth, so are my ways higher than your ways and my thoughts than your thoughts."* Our Father in Heaven wants to bless us exceedingly, abundantly above all we can ask or imagine. Our only part in that is to be specific, to never give up, and let God do the answering. Let's learn to be persistent, to demonstrate shameless audacity in making our requests known to God.

Bible Reading Plan: Luke 11:5-8 & Luke 18:1-8

Prayer Focus: As we come to the Lord today, let's ask Him to fill our heart with shameless audacity towards Him. Be unapologetic in your persistence towards things of God until you see the things of God manifest in your life. Be like the widow and demand that the Lord vindicate you of your enemy (the devil), for it is the enemy behind everything in your life that hinders the Will of God. Commit to pray through until you receive the promise.

Carolyn Olson

DAY 13 – BE RIGHTEOUS

Decide to be righteous. James 5:16 says, *"The prayer of a righteous person is powerful and effective."* In the NKJV, the scripture reads, *"The effective, fervent prayer of a righteous man avails much."* Many people read this and immediately look around for a righteous person to pray for them, wrongly thinking that the scripture refers to someone else. But what have we learned? We, as children of God, are the righteousness of God. It's because of Jesus, and the redemptive work of the cross, that brings us near the throne of God.

In Him, we live and move and have our being. (Acts 17:28)

In Him, we have eternal life. (John 3:15)

In Him, we are new creations with the life, nature, and ability of God. (2 Cor. 5:17)

In Him, we are His handiwork. (Eph. 2:10)

In Him, we are the righteousness of God (2 Cor. 5:21)

In Him, we are redeemed! (Col. 1:14 & Eph. 1:7)

In Him, we are called to holy life (2 Tim.1:9)

In Him, we are more than conquerors! (Rom. 8:37)

In Him, we can do all things through Him who gives us strength. (Phil. 4:13)

In Him, all spiritual blessings belong to us. (Eph. 1:3)

In Him, we are raised with Christ and sit with Him in the Heavenly realms. (Eph. 2:6)

In Him, God's promises are yes and amen! (2 Cor. 1:20)

In Him, we are righteous. In Him, the blessings of Abraham belong to us. We are that person mentioned in James 5:16. Knowing who we are in Christ enables us to come boldly to the throne and make our requests. Stand firm in who you are. You are the righteousness of God, in Christ. So, in Him, we can boldly come to God our Father knowing our fervent prayers are powerful and effective.

Bible Reading Plan: Romans 4

Prayer Focus: As you pray today, ask the Lord to show you how He sees you, and receive that knowledge deep in your heart. In prayer, decide to lay down all unbelief regarding the promises of God and by faith receive His Goodness for you, being fully persuaded that God has the power to do what He promises in His Word. Knowing that you are righteous in Him, and your prayers are powerful and effective, step out in faith and pray for someone else. Pray for your pastor, your team leader, your neighbor or co-worker and believe in your whole heart that what you are praying is powerful and effective.

Carolyn Olson

DAY 14 – PRAY EFFECTIVELY

Plan to pray effectively. James 5:16 says, "*The prayer of a righteous person is powerful and effective.*" In the NKJV, the scripture reads, "*The effective, fervent prayer of a righteous man avails much.*" Our prayers must be effective to avail much. Be intentional about praying effectively.

Your prayers are effective when you pray the will of God. Many Christians today lament not knowing the will of God. Their prayers are misguided as they seek healing for themselves or family members, help for financial lack, wisdom for relationships, etc. When the answer doesn't come within their own imposed timeline, they convince themselves that God's answer was no. Even worse, they tell themselves that their troubles are a thorn in their side, like Paul, or that God is just teaching them a lesson. In other words, they are settling for less than God's promises in His Word.

While it is true that God uses all circumstances, all things to work together for His good, He is a loving Father and He never changes. If He promised something in His Word, He would not change His mind to teach you a lesson. He will not impose on you things of the devil as chastisement. Satan is the god of this world and he is the enemy of our soul. Sickness, disease, pain, despair, and calamity are all of the devil, NOT of God. If you are amid something the devil put on you, then it is up to us, the believer, to do something about it. God has already done everything He's going to do about it. Our loving Father sent His Son, Jesus, as atonement for our sin. Jesus purchased our victory over sin and death. Further, Jesus has given us the keys to overcoming this dark world if we would only use them.

To pray effectively, we must always remember that we hold these keys, that we hold the Power of Attorney given to us by our Lord Jesus. 2 Corinthians 10: 4-5 says that *"the weapons of our warfare are not carnal but mighty in God for pulling down strongholds, casting down arguments and every high thing that exalts itself against the knowledge of God, bringing every thought into captivity to the obedience of Christ."* In prayer, we must take back what the devil has stolen from us. We must do it! The blessings of our Lord are there for us to receive, and the devil is right there too telling you that you can't have them. It's long past time to pick up our weapons and wage war for our families, our friends, and our church to take back what the devil has taken from us.

Understand that the Word of God is His Will. Jesus demonstrates the Will of God in action. Do you want to know the will of God? The read what Jesus said and did. It's all right there if you would only believe the Word of God. John 14:12 says, *"Very truly I tell you, whoever believes in me will do the works I have been doing, and they will do even greater things than these, because I am going to the Father."* What did Jesus do? He preached the gospel, healed the sick, cast out demons, performed signs and wonders, and demonstrated God's love wherever He went. Further, Mark 16:17-18 says, *"And these signs will accompany those who believe: In my name they will drive out demons; they will speak in new tongues; they will pick up snakes with their hands; and when they drink deadly poison, it will not hurt them at all; they will place their hands on sick people, and they will get well."*

What more do we need to believe God's Word is true for us believers today? It's time to start praying effective prayers by standing on the promises of God as outlined in His Word.

Bible Reading Plan: James 1 & James 5:13-20

Prayer Focus: As you pray today, earnestly seek to see His Word come to pass. Ask the Lord for His Power to rise within you to believe the Word as it is written. Let it be done! Pray for your family, your friends, and your church with this new-found belief that His Word is true. Use the weapons of your warfare and pull down the strongholds that have kept you from the blessings that rightfully belong to you. Believe it and receive it.

Carolyn Olson

DAY 15 – PRAY FERVENTLY

Commit to pray fervently. Pray boldly with the power and authority of the Word of God. James 5:16 says *"The effective, fervent prayer of a righteous man avails much."* We understand what it means to be effective, but what is fervency? According to Strong's Concordance, fervent means to "be mighty", "be at work", or "put forth power". As the righteous, children of God our prayers are effective and mighty, putting forth the power of God into any circumstance.

To intentionally pray fervently means to pray as if someone's life depended on it. Their life really does depend on your prayers, so we need to act like it. As believers, we need to stop pretending to pray and stop thinking someone else will pray. We see this on social media all the time. Something tragic happens, we see it posted, followed by a multitude of "praying for you" or "prayers". Truly, if that many children of God prayed, then that tragic event would be turned around in no time and we'd see more praise reports posted instead. Good intentions only go so far. I'm sure most everyone who posts "praying" intended to pray, but fell short of actually interceding for that person.

The challenge is to put action to our words. Praying fervently takes risks. Praying fervently takes our emotions and puts us in the place of that person or event we're seeking and may break our heart. We rise from our place of prayer in victory knowing with full assurance that our Father in Heaven heard us and is sending His answer. The answer may not be what we were thinking during prayer because His answers are always far abundantly more than we can ask or imagine.

John 15:7 says, "*If you remain in me and my words remain in you, ask whatever you wish, and it will be done for you.*" Knowing that you are praying God's Word, His Will, will powerfully ignite your prayers. Commit to taking a risk and pray fervently, standing on His Promises, and then rest in the absolute knowledge that what you've asked shall be done.

Bible Reading Plan: 1 Samuel 1:1-18

Prayer Focus: You may not be in deep anguish, but note Hannah's example; she was praying in her heart. As you pray today, consider Hannah's example of fervent prayer in 1 Samuel and pray from your heart for your church and community. Praying for the lost, the broken-hearted, the sick or the down-trodden, allow any feelings or emotions you feel to become part of your prayers. Lay it all out for the Lord, always standing on the Word in your requests and petitions.

Carolyn Olson

DAY 16 – RECEIVE ALL THAT JESUS PURCHASED FOR YOU

By faith, receive all that is rightfully yours in Christ Jesus. In Luke 4:18-19 Jesus says, "The Spirit of the Lord is upon me, because He has anointed me to preach the gospel to the poor; He has sent me to heal the brokenhearted, to proclaim liberty to the captives and recovery of sight to the blind, to set at liberty those who are oppressed; to proclaim the acceptable year of the Lord."

This scripture clearly outlines the work of Jesus and what He purchased for us:

1. Jesus was anointed to preach the gospel to the poor. The poor means us. It means you and me and your neighbors and friends who don't know the Lord. It means the lowly and afflicted. Therefore, receive this gospel that Jesus preached.

2. Jesus was sent to heal the brokenhearted. Jesus was set apart to make whole those whose heart has been shattered and crushed by this world. If your thoughts or feelings have ever

been shattered and broken apart, then receive your healing from the One set apart to restore you.

3. Jesus was sent to proclaim liberty to the captives. The word 'captives' here literally means "prisoner of war". Before we knew Him, we were captives of this world held in sin and ruled by the devil. But Jesus came to set us free! He proclaimed freedom to the prisoners! Let's intentionally receive this freedom and truly live our lives free from the chains that used to bind us.

4. Jesus was sent to recover sight to the blind. Figuratively and literally, Jesus was sent to restore sight to the physically and mentally blind. Receive this restoration of sight, so we are no longer physically or mentally blind to His Truth.

5. Jesus was sent to set at liberty those who are oppressed. He was sent to release from bondage those who are oppressed, crushed or bruised. Receive your freedom!

6. Jesus was sent to proclaim the acceptable year of the Lord. He was sent to proclaim <u>now</u> is the time for His favor. Receive this charge that <u>now</u> is the time to act.

Jesus is standing at the door to our hearts bearing gifts if we would only receive them. Looking at this from God's perspective, our Father sent His ONLY SON to be sacrificed for our redemption, for the forgiveness of our sin, while we were still sinners. He sent His ONLY SON, to be beaten and bruised for our healing. His ONLY SON willingly bore our sin, shame, weaknesses, diseases, addictions, burdens, trials, pain, depression, anxiety, worry, heartache, grief...Jesus bore it all for us, yet many times we cling to the former way or our former life not fully receiving ALL that He bought for us.

It's not like we intentionally refuse the gifts of Jesus. Sometimes it is ignorance of the Word that prevents us from living the life of abundance and victory that He intended for His children. Most times it's the enemy of our souls that cheats us out of our inheritance. The devil comes to steal, kill and destroy God's children. How long are we going to let the devil steal God's blessings from us? How long will we let the devil steal our health, our finances, or our peace? As children of God, let's educate ourselves in His Word and learn His Will for our lives. Let's set out to receive God's blessings and all that Jesus purchased for us and take back what the devil has stolen from us.

He is such a good, good Father! Let's choose to believe that He will do immeasurably more than all we ask or imagine.

Bible Reading Plan: Romans 8:1-17

Prayer Focus: Prayerfully reflect on the reading passage today in Romans 8. Ask our Father to give you a deeper revelation of the Spirit of Christ within you, to know deep down in your heart that as children of God we are heirs of God and co-heirs with Christ. Ask the Father to ready your heart and mind to receive all His Blessings, to receive the freedom that is found in Christ alone, and to understand deep in our inner being that the Spirit of God who raised Jesus from the dead lives inside of us, to give LIFE to our mortal bodies.

DAY 17 – RECEIVE THE HOLY SPIRIT

Choose to receive the Holy Spirit. Being saved means, we are born again and have received new life in Christ. John 3:5-6 explains that to enter the Kingdom of God we are born of water and the Spirit, and that Spirit gives birth to spirit. Every believer has the Holy Spirit in a measure through the new birth, through salvation. But there is a work of the Spirit that the Father wants to work in all His children after salvation, after being born again, and that is the infilling of the Holy Spirit mentioned in Luke 24:49 and Acts 1:8.

Luke 24:49 says, "*I am going to send you what my Father has promised; but stay in the city until you have been clothed with power from on high.*" Jesus promised to send what the Father promised describing it as being "*clothed with power from on high.*" Acts 1:8 says, "*But you will receive power when the Holy Spirit comes on you.*" The events in Acts 2 are described here. The Holy Spirit was given on the Day of Pentecost, and He's been here ever since that day. The Holy Spirit was given once, and it is up to us to receive Him.

We see a picture of this in Acts 8:15-17, *"When they arrived, they prayed for the new believers there that they might receive the Holy Spirit, because the Holy Spirit had not yet come on any of them; they had simply been baptized in the name of the Lord Jesus. Then Peter and John placed their hands on them, and they received the Holy Spirit."* The Samaritan Christians had received their salvation and been baptized with water, but they had not yet received the Holy Spirit. So, Peter and John laid hands on them and then they received the Holy Spirit. This greater enduement of power by the infilling of the Holy Spirit is for believers today. There is no reason to wait, and no preparation is needed. Getting saved gets you ready! According to Acts 2:39 the only requirement is being saved. If you are a born-again believer and sincerely seek to be filled with the Holy Spirit, it will be done. Luke 11:13 says, *"If you then, though you are evil, know how to give good gifts to your children, how much more will your Father in heaven give the Holy Spirit to those who ask him!"*

Receive is an active word meaning to come into possession of something. When you first received your salvation, you received the Word gladly, proclaimed with your mouth Jesus is Lord and received your salvation by faith. The same is true here: receive the Holy Spirit, just as you received salvation....by faith. And how will you know that you've been filled with the Spirit? Acts 2:4 answers clearly, *"All of them were filled with the Holy Spirit and began to speak in other tongues as the Spirit enabled them."* You will know you have been baptized in the Holy Spirit by the Biblical evidence of speaking in tongues. Now this speaking in tongues is not to be confused with the gifts of the Spirit. There is a difference between the Biblical evidence of the infilling of the Spirit (Acts 2) and the gift of tongues (1 Cor. 12).

Every believer that is baptized in the Holy Spirit will have the evidence of speaking in tongues based on Acts 2:4, which is the original pattern of being filled. Acts 10:44-48 is further evidence that speaking in tongues is proof of the Holy Spirit's infilling because it was tongues that convinced the Jews that the Holy Spirit had filled the Gentiles, that salvation was for the Gentiles and the Jews. Finally, Acts 19:6 gives us further evidence that tongues follow the infilling of the Spirit, *"When Paul placed his hands on them, the Holy Spirit came on them, and they spoke in tongues and prophesied."*

Bible Reading Plan: Acts 2

Prayer Focus: As you pray today, yield yourself for God to fill. Lay aside all preconceived notions and seek to receive ALL that God has for you. Ask to be filled with the Spirit, to be filled with the promised Power from on High. Apply what you've learned in the Word – ask and it shall be given, if you believe. Ask, believe, receive. Then open your mouth in faith and give praise to the Only One who does abundantly more than all we ask or imagine.

Carolyn Olson

DAY 18 – RELY ON THE HOLY SPIRIT TO HELP YOU PRAY

Determine to rely on the Holy Spirit to help you pray. Being baptized in the Holy Spirit gives us access to the Power of God inside of us, for this is our inheritance. The accompanying evidence of speaking in tongues has many purposes in our personal prayer life. 1 Corinthians 14:2 says, *"For anyone who speaks in a tongue does not speak to people but to God. Indeed, no one understands them; they utter mysteries by the Spirit."* Wow! Did you catch that? Praying in tongues is directly speaking to God uttering *"mysteries by the Spirit."* Romans 8:26 says, *"In the same way, the Spirit helps us in our weakness. We do not know what we ought to pray for, but the Spirit himself intercedes for us through wordless groans."* Being filled with the Spirit, and praying in the Spirit, allows supernatural intercession to flow through us.

Yielding ourselves to the Holy Spirit in prayer allows the Power of God to ignite our prayer life. We do not know how to pray, but the Holy Spirit prays for us. This is powerful! This is effective!

Truly, how can our human mind comprehend the mysteries of God and know how to pray effectively in all circumstances? We can't. So, God gave the promised Holy Spirit to teach us all things and to remind us of what is said in His Word. The Holy Spirit will guide us into all Truth so as we pray for ourselves, our families, our church, our neighbors, or our communities, our prayers will be guided into all Truth assuring us that our prayers are effective.

Ephesians 6:18 says, *"And pray in the Spirit on all occasions with all kinds of prayers and requests. With this in mind, be alert and always keep on praying for all the Lord's people."* Praying in the Spirit is the only way to *"be alert and keep on praying"*.

Bible Reading Plan: 1 Corinthians 14:1-25

Prayer Focus: As you pray today, reflect on this passage in 1 Corinthians 14 and seek to do our part in becoming the church Paul described. Let's earnestly seek God to be the one who prophesies, speaking to people for their strengthening, encouraging and comfort. Let's ask God to use each of us to prophesy strength, encouragement and comfort to each other, not in tongues but still under the unction of the Holy Spirit. Earnestly ask God to bring unbelievers to church so that while we are encouraging one another with prophesy, their hearts would be laid bare and they would fall and worship God proclaiming, "God is really among you!"

Carolyn Olson

DAY 19 – MAKE INTERCESSION FOR OTHERS

Choose to make intercession for others. Intercession means the act of intervening on behalf of another. The greatest act of love you can do for your neighbor is to pray for them, to stand in the gap, asking God to intervene in their lives. Interceding for others is something every believer can do from the first day they are saved. Asking God to honor His Promises for someone else is an act of worship. We honor Him when we allow His Love to flow through us in prayer as we seek His Face on behalf of someone else.

There are times in our lives where our circumstances seem larger than life. During those valleys, it's all we can do to move through the day barely able to care for ourselves. It is times like this that we desperately need someone willing to hold us up in prayer. When we can't do it ourselves, when we feel crushed by our circumstances, we need the intervention, the intercession, of other believers.

Ezekiel 22:30 says, "*I looked for someone among them who would build up the wall and stand before me in the gap on behalf of the land, so I would not have to destroy it, but I found no one.*" This passage about Jerusalem reveals that God wants to help and change circumstances, but He's looking for someone to "stand in the gap" so He wouldn't destroy it. As we look around at our families, church, communities, and nation, we can't help but see the devastation that is lurking trying to overtake us.

Are we willing to be that one person to build up the wall and stand before God in the gap on behalf of others? Our Father needs his children to be willing to give their time, to pray and allow their heart to be broken for someone else. It only takes a few minutes to say a few sentences in faith, in the Name of Jesus, to change someone's life.

Bible Reading Plan: Genesis 18:22-33

Prayer Focus: As you pray today, ask the Lord to give you the heart of an intercessor. Ask Him to fill you with the confidence of Abraham as you enter His Presence to stand in the gap for someone else. Allow the Holy Spirit to lead you; pray for that person whatever comes from you heart and remember to be specific. Pray fervently for them, knowing that your prayers are powerful and effective.

DAY 20 – WAGE WAR AGAINST YOUR ENEMY

Willfully wage war against your enemy. Ephesians 6:12 (KJV) says, "For we wrestle not against flesh and blood, but against principalities, against powers, against the rulers of the darkness of this world, against spiritual wickedness in high places." Never forget that our trials and tribulations are not against people, but against the god of this world. 1 Peter 5:8 says, "Be alert and of sober mind. Your enemy, the devil, prowls around like a roaring lion looking for someone to devour."

All too many times we get caught up in the emotion of the moment and blame people for difficulties. Jealous, envy and strife follow us around trying to get us to see the problem is with the natural world or with people instead of seeing the truth - that the devil wants to destroy you. Although he's already lost the war, the devil continually tries to convince us that there is no war, that "that's just the way things are". The devil's worst lie is that God allows these bad things in our lives to teach us a lesson. Yes, all things work together for good, for those who love God and are called according to his purpose. Miraculously yes, God takes the sin and the yuck of this world and uses them for good. But He doesn't bring the sin and the yuck. God won't put on you what is of the devil. If God is putting on you the trials, the tribulations, the diseases and pains of this world, then He's a liar and He really didn't send Jesus to vindicate us from all that. God will never go back on His Word, and His Word is clear that He sent Jesus to rescue us and set us free from the bonds of the devil. Never forget this spiritual battle.

So how do we wage this spiritual battle? What are the weapons of our warfare? The answer is found in Ephesians 6. Actually, the entire book of Ephesians is one of edifying the church and building up the body of believers into knowing their inheritance as children of God. The armor described in Ephesians 6:14-17 is put on in prayer, like this:

1. Put on the belt of truth – Get a clear understanding of God's Word
2. Put on the breastplate of righteousness – Put on Jesus, our righteousness and our obedience to God's Word
3. Fit your feet with the preparation of the gospel of peace – Have faithful ministry proclaiming the Word of God
4. Pick up the shield of faith – Declare complete safety under the blood of Christ
5. Put on the helmet of salvation – Protect your head from turning from the truth
6. Pick up and use the sword of the Spirit – The Word of God; use the Word offensively in the battle against evil

The real power is understanding Ephesians 6:13, which says, *"Therefore put on the full armor of God, so that when the day of evil comes, you may be able to stand your ground, and after you have done everything, to stand."* We put on this armor to stand our ground against the devil. And after we have done all, we stand. To *stand* means to uphold or sustain the authority! That's right...we stand against the devil with all authority over him. Remember, we have the power of attorney from our Lord Jesus. In His Name, we can move mountains. In His Name we pray, "Thy Kingdom come! Thy Will be done on Earth as it is in Heaven!" in full assurance and confidence that praying His Word, His Will, is heard and answered.

Bible Reading Plan: Ephesians 6

Prayer Focus: In prayer today, put on the full armor of God and take your stand against the enemy of your soul, against the enemy of your family and friends. As you pray and intercede for your pastor and the church, remember that the battle isn't against people, but against the devil and demons that would try to trip you up. Take your stand, uphold the authority given you by Jesus Christ and send those demons packing! Whether it's sickness or poverty, in His Name, break that power and claim the victory that is only found in Jesus.

Carolyn Olson

DAY 21 – ABOVE ALL ELSE, GIVE PRAISE AND THANKSGIVING

Determine in your heart to give praise and thanksgiving regardless of your circumstance. 1 Thess. 5:18 says to *"give thanks in all circumstances; for this is God's will for you in Christ Jesus."* And Philippians 4:6-7 says, *"Do not be anxious about anything, but in every situation, by prayer and petition, with thanksgiving, present your requests to God. And the peace of God, which transcends all understanding, will guard your hearts and your minds in Christ Jesus."*

While God commands us to give praise and thanksgiving, the reality is that sometimes we don't want to do it. When disappointments come, and our hearts are heavy, we don't feel joyful or thankful. It is far easier to see your situation in all its bleakness instead of seeing it from God's perspective. But that is just what praising Him will do for you. Praise changes your perspective.

Praising God gets the focus off ourselves and back on Him. When we're wallowing in our sorrow, it is a very selfish place to be. All the focus tends to be on us, while praising Him puts the focus squarely back on God. Isaiah 43:2 says, *"When you pass through the waters, I will be with you; and when you pass through the rivers, they will not sweep over you. When you walk through the fire, you will not be burned; the flames will not set you ablaze."* Knowing that regardless of how circumstances look, God never fails.

Remember Paul and Silas praising God in prison until an earthquake freed them. (Acts 16). Their circumstances were very bleak, having been beaten with rods, and their feet fastened in the stocks in the inner cell. How miserable they must have been, both physically and mentally! Yet, they praised God during their pain and suffering. As a result, they were freed, and the jailor came to know Christ. It didn't just happen for them. Paul and Silas had a choice to make, and they chose to praise God despite their circumstances. Let's learn from their example, being all strengthened with the power of the Holy Spirit, and decide to praise God amid our suffering.

Bible Reading Plan: Acts 16:16–40

Prayer Focus: Give thanks and praise God this day for all that He's done. There really are no human words adequate to express just how awesome, amazing and holy is our God! Pray in the Spirit. Let your whole being rejoice and give thanks. Remind the Lord of all the prayers spoken over the last 20 days. Be like Jesus in John 11:41 and say, "Father, I thank You that You have heard me." in full assurance that our Father in Heaven has answered.

Carolyn Olson

PRAYER JOURNAL:

_____
_____
_____
_____
_____
_____
_____
_____
_____
_____
_____
_____
_____
_____
_____
_____
_____
_____
_____
_____
_____
_____

Made in the USA
Middletown, DE
14 February 2018